# Education
## Free & Compulsory

Murray N. Rothbard

Ludwig von Mises Institute
Auburn, Alabama

This work was originally published in the April and July–August 1971 issues of *The Individualist*, and then revised and published by the Center for Independent Education in 1979. This edition restores the original text. Thanks to Mises Institute summer fellow Candice Jackson for editorial assistance, and to Institute Member Richard Perry for the index.

The US government's World War II school propaganda poster, reproduced on the cover, is an apt illustration of the State's ideal for education.

Published by the Ludwig von Mises Institute, 518 West Magnolia Avenue, Auburn, Alabama 36832-4528.

ISBN: 0945466-22-6

# TABLE OF CONTENTS

# Preface

The central concern of social theory and policy in the new millennium should be to redefine fundamentally the role of the state in its relations to individuals, families, communities. This must also include a rethinking of the means, methods, and institutions most suitable for the education of the child.

What urgently requires correction is today's dramatic imbalance between families and the state. It is an imbalance that overwhelmingly favors the controlling power of the political sphere relative to that of parents and children to seek out educational settings that are best suited to the full educational development of the individual.

What is at stake is nothing less than the very concept of what it means to live and thrive as a human being. Must people be controlled and coerced from the cradle by enormous political bureaucracies with preset agendas on who may teach and how, what we must learn and when? Or can people generally work out for themselves what is in their best interests and seek ways to make their interests consistent with the common good, rightly understood?

Another way to put the question is framed up perfectly in Murray N. Rothbard's resplendent manifesto: is education to be conducted in an institutional setting of freedom, or must it be compulsorily financed and administered? It is an old question that dates back to the very beginnings of political philosophy, but one that is rarely discussed today, though it becomes especially pertinent in this time of rising violence and declining values in our public educational institutions.

To decide that government and not the family has the primary responsibility for overseeing the education of the child may, at first, appear to be a small concession. But as we have seen in this century, it is not easy—and may in fact be impossible—to rein in political power once it gains control over schooling. Since the early 1930s, when the federal and state government became more aggressively involved in education, control has become incrementally more centralized.

For instance, in the year of my birth, 1932, there were 128,000 school districts in the United States, while today there are less than 15,000. This shrinkage and centralization of decisionmaking has gone on at the same time our student population has grown to twice the size. This is to say nothing of the hundreds of billions of dollars, taken from taxpayers and spent by local, state, and federal government on education, the result of which has been only to diminish the quality of their output.

Moreover, and exactly as Rothbard predicted nearly three decades ago, these institutions are increasingly imposing politicized, standardized, one-size-fits-all curricula that neither accommodate individual strengths nor correct for individual weaknesses. Before "Goals 2000" and its dubious predecessors, Rothbard foresaw the way in which schools are used to impose a political agenda that in turn seeks to reinforce political support for official institutions. Many years before the astonishing increase in home-schooling, he argued that the ideal education was one-on-one, supervised by the parent.

Education continues to be one of the most politically charged issues in our national culture, and the conflicts over education in America are likely to grow more polarized so long as the political control grows ever tighter. Indeed, for centuries the political control of education has engendered social conflict, and even led to civil wars and revolutions. Isn't it time this system be completely rethought along the lines Professor Rothbard discusses? I believe so.

Despite all the talk about education reform, now decades running, this debate has not yet begun, primarily because the topical boundaries have been too narrowly drawn. With his sweeping and unflinchingly radical rethinking of the very structure of educational institutions, Professor Rothbard shocks us out of our stupor and calls us toward the total reconceptualization that is more necessary than ever.

Kevin Ryan
*Emeritus Professor of Education*
Director, Center for the Advancement of Ethics and Character
Boston University

# The Individual's Education

Every human infant comes into the world devoid of the faculties characteristic of fully-developed human beings. This does not mean simply the ability to see clearly, to move around, to feed oneself, etc.; above all, it means he is devoid of reasoning power—the power that distinguishes man from animals. But the crucial distinction between the baby and other animals is that these powers, in particular the ability to reason, are potentially within him. The process of growing up is the process of the development of the child's faculties. From a state of helplessness and incompetence such as few newly-born animals are burdened with, the infant grows up to the glory of the full stature of an adult.

Because they are immediately apparent to the senses, it is easy to overestimate the purely physical nature of these changes; the baby's growth in height and weight, learning how to walk and talk, etc., may be viewed in terms of the isolated physical or muscular activities involved. The overwhelmingly important feature of the growing-up process is mental, the development of mental powers, or perception and reason. The child using the new mental powers learns and acquires knowledge—knowledge not only about the world around him, but also about himself. Thus, his learning to walk and talk and his direction of these powers depends upon his mental capacity to acquire this knowledge, and to use it. As the child exercises his new reasoning, as well as muscular powers, these powers grow and develop, which in turn furnishes an impetus for the child's further exercise of these faculties. Specifically, the child learns about the world around him, other children and adults, and his own mental and physical powers.

Every child coming into the world comes into a certain environment. This environment consists of physical things, natural and man-made, and other human beings with whom he comes in contact in various ways. It is this environment upon which he exercises his developing powers. His reason forms judgments about other people, about his relationships with them and with the world in general; his reason reveals to him his own desires and his physical powers. In this way, the growing child, working with his environment, develops ends and discovers means to achieve them. His ends are based on his own personality, the moral principles he has concluded are best, and his aesthetic tastes; his knowledge of means is based on what he has learned is most appropriate. This body of "theory" in which he believes, he has acquired with his reasoning powers, either from the direct experience of himself or others, or from logical deduction by himself or by others. When he finally reaches adulthood, he has developed his faculties to whatever extent he can, and has acquired a set of values, principles, and scientific knowledge.

This entire process of growing up, of developing all the facets of a man's personality, is his education. It is obvious that a person acquires his education in all activities of his childhood; all his waking hours are spent in learning in one form or another.[1] It is clearly absurd to limit the term "education" to a person's formal schooling. He is learning all the time. He learns and forms ideas about other people, their desires, and actions to achieve them, the world and the natural laws that govern it; and his own ends, and how to achieve them. He formulates ideas on the nature of man, and what his own and others' ends should be in light of this nature. This is a continual process, and it is obvious that formal schooling constitutes only an item in this process.

In a fundamental sense, as a matter of fact, everyone is "self-educated." A person's environment, physical or social, does not "determine" the ideas and knowledge with which he will emerge as an adult. It is a fundamental fact of human nature that a person's ideas are formed for himself; others may influence them, but none can determine absolutely the ideas and values which the individual will adopt or maintain through life.

---

[1]Adults, too, are engaged in learning throughout their lives, about themselves, other people, and the world. However, since their reasoning powers, in contrast to the child's, are already developed, they will not be discussed here.

## Formal Instruction

If everyone is constantly learning, and each child's life is his education, why the need for formal education? The need for formal instruction stems from the fact that a child's faculties are undeveloped and only potential, and that they need experience in order to develop. In order for this exercise to take place, the child needs the environmental materials on which he can operate, and with which he can work. Now it is clear that for a large segment of his general education, he does not need systematic, formal instruction. The space is almost always available for his physical faculties to develop and exercise. For this, no formal instruction is needed. If food and shelter are provided for him, he will grow physically without much instruction. His relationships with others—members of the family and outsiders—will develop spontaneously in the process of living. In all of these matters, a child will spontaneously exercise his faculties on these materials abundant in the world around him. Those precepts that are needed can be imparted relatively simply, without need for systematic study.

But there is one area of education where direct spontaneity and a few precepts will not suffice. This is the area of formal study, specifically the area of intellectual knowledge. That knowledge beyond the direct area of his daily life involves a far greater exercise of reasoning powers. This knowledge must be imparted by the use of observation and deductive reasoning, and such a body of thought takes a good deal of time to learn. Furthermore, it must be learned systematically, since reasoning proceeds in orderly, logical steps, organizing observation into a body of systematic knowledge.

The child, lacking the observations and the developed reasoning powers, will never learn these subjects by himself alone, as he can other things. He could not observe and deduce them by his own unaided mental powers. He may learn them from the oral explanations of an instructor, or from the written testimony of books, or from a combination of both. The advantage of the book is that it can set forth the subject fully and systematically; the advantage of the teacher is that, in addition to previous knowledge from the book, he knows and deals with the child directly, and can explain the salient or unclear points. Generally, it has been found that a combination of book and teacher is best for formal instruction.

Formal instruction, therefore, deals with the body of knowledge on certain definite subjects. These subjects are: first of all, reading, so that the child has a superb tool for future acquisition of knowledge, and as a later corollary, the various "language arts" such as spelling and grammar. Writing is another powerful key in the child's mental development. After these tools are mastered, instruction naturally proceeds in logical development: reading to be spent on such subjects as the world's natural laws (natural science); the record of man's development, his ends and actions (history, geography); and later the "moral sciences" of human behavior (economics, politics, philosophy, psychology); and man's imaginative studies of man (literature). Writing branches out into essays on these various subjects, and into composition. A third elementary tool of great power is arithmetic, beginning with simple numbers and leading up into more developed branches of mathematics. Of these fundamental subjects, reading is of first importance, and for this learning of the alphabet is the primary and logical tool.

It has become fashionable to deride stress of the "three Rs," but it is obvious that they are of enormous importance, that the sooner they are thoroughly learned, the sooner the child will be able to absorb the vast area of knowledge that constitutes the great heritage of human civilization. They are the keys that unlock the doors of human knowledge, and the doors to the flowering and development of the child's mental powers. It is also clear that the only necessity and use for systematic formal teaching arises in these technical subjects, since knowledge of them must be presented systematically. There is clearly no need for formal instruction in "how to play," in "getting along with the group," in "selecting a dentist," and the multitude of similar "courses" given in "modern education." And, since there is no need for formal teaching in physical or directly spontaneous areas, there is no need for instruction in "physical education" or in finger-painting.[2]

## Human Diversity and Individual Instruction

One of the most important facts about human nature is the great diversity among individuals. Of course, there are certain

---

[2]Later on in life, of course, the youth may well take specific courses in athletics, painting, or music, but this is far different, since it would be systematic study of the subject as a specialty.

broad characteristics, physical and mental, which are common to all human beings.[3] But more than any other species, individual men are distinct and separate individuals. Not only is each fingerprint unique, each personality is unique as well. Each person is unique in his tastes, interests, abilities, and chosen activities. Animal activities, routine and guided by instinct, tend to be uniform and alike. But human individuals, despite similarities in ends and values, despite mutual influences, tend to express the unique imprint of the individual's own personality. The development of individual variety tends to be both the cause and the effect of the progress of civilization. As civilization progresses, there is more opportunity for the development of a person's reasoning and tastes in a growing variety of fields. And from such opportunities come the advancement of knowledge and progress which in turn add to the society's civilization. Furthermore, it is the variety of individual interests and talents that permits the growth of specialization and division of labor, on which civilized economies depend. As the Reverend George Harris expressed it:

> Savagery is uniformity. The principal distinctions are sex, age, size, and strength. Savages...think alike or not at all, and converse therefore in monosyllables. There is scarcely any variety, only a horde of men, women, and children. The next higher stage, which is called barbarism, is marked by increased variety of functions. There is some division of labor, some interchange of thought, better leadership, more intellectual and aesthetic cultivation. The highest stage, which is called civilization, shows the greatest degree of specialization. Distinct functions become more numerous. Mechanical, commercial, educational, scientific, political, and artistic occupations multiply. The rudimentary societies are characterized by the likeness of equality; the developed societies are marked by the unlikeness of inequality or variety. As we go down, monotony; as we go up, variety. As we go down, persons are more alike; as we go up, persons are more unlike, it certainly seems...as though [the] approach to equality is decline towards the conditions of savagery, and as though variety is an advance towards higher civilization....
>
> Certainly, then, if progress is to be made by added satisfactions, there must be even more variety of functions,

---

[3]For further writings on the topics of biological individuality and psychology see Roger J. Williams, *Free and Unequal* (1953), and *Biochemical Individuality* (1956); Gordon W. Allport, *Becoming* (1955); and Abraham H. Maslow, *Toward a Psychology of Being* (1962).

> new and finer differentiations of training and pursuits.
> Every step of progress means the addition of a human
> factor that is in some way unlike all existing factors. The
> progress of civilization, then...must be an increasing
> diversification of the individuals that compose society....
> There must be articulation of each new invention and art,
> of fresh knowledge, and of broader application of moral
> principles.[4]

With the development of civilization and individual diversity, there is less and less area of identical uniformity, and therefore less "equality." Only robots on the assembly line or blades of grass can be considered as completely equal, as being identical with respect to all of their attributes. The fewer attributes that two organisms have in common, the less they are "equal" and the more they are unequal. Civilized human beings, therefore, are unequal in most of their personalities. This fact of inequality, in tastes, and in ability and character, is not necessarily an invidious distinction. It simply reflects the scope of human diversity.

It is evident that the common enthusiasm for equality is, in the fundamental sense, anti-human. It tends to repress the flowering of individual personality and diversity, and civilization itself; it is a drive toward savage uniformity. Since abilities and interests are naturally diverse, a drive toward making people equal in all or most respects is necessarily a leveling downward. It is a drive against development of talent, genius, variety, and reasoning power. Since it negates the very principles of human life and human growth, the creed of equality and uniformity is a creed of death and destruction.

There is a sense, however, in which equality among men is sensible and beneficial. Each individual should have the freest possible scope for the development of his faculties and his personality. In order to have this scope, he must have freedom from violence against himself. Violence can only repress and destroy human growth and endeavor, and neither can reason and creativity function under an atmosphere of coercion. If each person has equal defense against violence, this "equality before the law" will permit him to maximize his potentialities.

Since each person is a unique individual, it is clear that the best type of formal instruction is that type which is suited to his own

---

[4]George Harris, *Inequality and Progress* (Boston: Houghton, Mifflin, 1898), pp. 74–75, 88 and passim.

particular individuality. Each child has different intelligence, aptitudes, and interests. Therefore, the best choice of pace, timing, variety, and manner, and of the courses of instruction will differ widely from one child to another. One child is best suited, in interests and ability, for an intensive course in arithmetic three times a week, followed six months later by a similar course in reading; another may require a brief period of several courses; a third may need a lengthy period of instruction in reading, etc. Given the formal, systematic courses of instruction, there is an infinite variety of pace and combination which may be most suitable for each particular child.

It is obvious, therefore, that the best type of instruction is individual instruction. A course where one teacher instructs one pupil is clearly by far the best type of course. It is only under such conditions that human potentialities can develop to their greatest degree. It is clear that the formal school, characterized by classes in which one teacher instructs many children, is an immensely inferior system. Since each child differs from the other in interest and ability, and the teacher can only teach one thing at a time, it is evident that every school class must cast all the instruction into one uniform mold. Regardless how the teacher instructs, at what pace, timing, or variety, he is doing violence to each and every one of the children. Any schooling involves misfitting each child into a Procrustean bed of unsuitable uniformity.

What then shall we say of laws imposing compulsory schooling on every child? These laws are endemic in the Western world. In those places where private schools are allowed, they must all meet standards of instruction imposed by the government. Yet the injustice of imposing any standards of instruction should be clear. Some children are duller and should be instructed at a slower pace; the bright children require a rapid pace to develop their faculties. Furthermore, many children are very apt in one subject and very dull in another. They should certainly be permitted to develop themselves in their best subjects and to drop the poor ones. Whatever the standards that the government imposes for instruction, injustice is done to all—to the dullards who cannot absorb any instruction, to those with different sets of aptitudes in different subjects, to the bright children whose minds would like to be off and winging in more advanced courses but who must wait until the dullards are hounded once again. Similarly, any pace that the teacher sets in class wreaks an injustice on almost all; on the dull who cannot keep up, and on the bright who lose interest and precious chances to develop their great potential.

Obviously, the worst injustice is the prevention of parental teaching of their own children. Parental instruction conforms to the ideal arrangement. It is, first of all, individualized instruction, the teacher dealing directly with the unique child, and addressing himself to his capabilities and interests. Second, what people can know the aptitudes and personality of the child better than his own parents? The parents' daily familiarity with, and love for, their children, renders them uniquely qualified to give the child the formal instruction necessary. Here the child receives individual attention for his own personality. No one is as qualified as the parent to know how much or at what pace he should teach the child, what the child's requirements are for freedom or guidance, etc.

Almost all parents are qualified to teach their children, particularly in the elementary subjects. Those who are not so qualified in the subjects can hire individual tutors for their children. Tutors may also be hired where the parents do not have the time to devote to the formal instruction of their children. Whether or not they themselves should do the teaching, or which tutor is the best for their child, is best determined under the overall supervision of the parents directly. The parents can determine the progress of the child, the daily effect of the tutor on the child, etc.

In addition to parental instruction and tutorial instruction, the parents can send the children to private schools. This alternative, however, is not as satisfactory because of the necessary lack of individual instruction and individual pacing. There are classes with many children, set times for courses, set grades, etc. The only reason for schools instead of individual instruction is the economic one: that the price of individual tutoring is prohibitive for most parents. Consequently, they must adopt the only practical alternative of mass tutoring, where the teacher instructs many children at the same time. It is clear that such private schools are an inferior solution to individual instruction. Whichever pace the teacher sets, an injustice is done to many of the children. If the State enforces certain "standards" on the private schools, a far worse crime against the children is committed. For if the parents' selection of instruction is completely free and unhampered by State coercion, they, knowing and loving the child best, will be able to select the best type of instruction that they can afford. If they hire tutors, they will choose the most competent for their child. If they can select any type of private school, they will select that type which is best suited for their child. The advantages of unlimited development of private schools is that there will tend to be developed on the free market a different type of school for each type of demand. Schools will tend to be developed especially for bright children, for average children, and for dull ones, for those with broad aptitudes, and for those for whom it would be best to specialize, etc. But if the State decrees that there may be no schools which do not, for example, teach arithmetic, it would mean that those children who may be bright in other subjects but have little or no aptitude for arithmetic will have to be subjected to needless suffering. The State's imposition of uniform standards does grave violation to the diversity of human tastes and abilities.

The effect of the State's compulsory schooling laws is not only to repress the growth of specialized, partly individualized, private schools for the needs of various types of children. It also prevents the education of the child by the people who, in many respects, are best qualified—his parents. The effect is also to force into schools children who have little or no aptitude for instruction at all. It so happens that among the variety of human ability there is a large number of subnormal children, children who are not receptive to instruction, whose reasoning capacity is not too great. To force these children to be exposed to schooling, as the State does almost everywhere, is a criminal offense to their natures. Without the ability to learn systematic subjects, they must either sit and suffer while others learn, or the bright and average students must be held back greatly in their development while these children are pressured to learn. In any case, the instruction has almost no effect on these children, many of whose hours of life are simply wasted because of the State's decree. If these hours were spent in simple, direct experience which they were better able to absorb, there is no question that they would be healthier children and adults as a result. But to dragoon them into a school for a formative decade of their lives, to force them to attend classes in which they have no interest or ability, is to warp their entire personalities.

## The Parent or the State

The key issue in the entire discussion is simply this: shall the parent or the State be the overseer of the child? An essential feature of human life is that, for many years, the child is relatively helpless, that his powers of providing for himself mature late. Until these powers are fully developed he cannot act completely for himself as a responsible individual. He must be under tutelage. This tutelage is a complex and difficult task. From an infancy of complete dependence and subjection to adults, the child must grow up gradually to the status of an independent adult. The question is under whose guidance, and virtual "ownership" the child should be: his parents' or the State's? There is no third, or middle, ground in this issue. Some party must control, and no one suggests that some individual third party have authority to seize the child and rear it.

It is obvious that the natural state of affairs is for the parents to have charge of the child. The parents are the literal producers of the child, and the child is in the most intimate relationship to them that any people can be to one another. The parents have ties of family affection to the child. The parents are interested in the child as an individual, and are the most likely to be interested and familiar with his requirements and personality. Finally, if one believes at all in a free society, where each one owns himself and his own products, it is obvious that his own child, one of his most precious products, also comes under his charge.

The only logical alternative to parental "ownership" of the child is for the State to seize the infant from the parents and to rear it completely itself. To any believer in freedom this must seem a monstrous step indeed. In the first place, the rights of the parents are completely violated, their own loving product seized from them to be subjected to the will of strangers. In the second place, the rights of the child are violated, for he grows up in subjection to the unloving hands of the State, with little regard for his individual personality. Furthermore—and this is a most important consideration—for each person to be "educated," to develop his faculties to the fullest, he needs freedom for this development. We have seen above that freedom from violence is essential to the development of a man's reason and personality. But the State! The State's very being rests on violence, on compulsion. As a matter of fact, the very feature that distinguishes the State from other individuals and groups is that the State has the only (legal) power to use violence. In contrast to all other individuals and organizations, the State issues decrees which must be obeyed at the risk of suffering prison or the electric chair. The child would have to grow up under the wings of an institution resting on violence and restriction. What sort of peaceful development could take place under such auspices?

Furthermore, it is inevitable that the State would impose uniformity on the teaching of charges. Not only is uniformity more congenial to the bureaucratic temper and easier to enforce; this would be almost inevitable where collectivism has supplanted individualism. With collective State ownership of the children replacing individual ownership and rights, it is clear that the collective principle would be enforced in teaching as well. Above all, what would be taught is the doctrine of obedience to the State itself. For tyranny is not really congenial to the spirit of man, who requires freedom for his full development.

Therefore, techniques of inculcating reverence for despotism and other types of "thought control" are bound to emerge. Instead of spontaneity, diversity, and independent men, there would emerge a race of passive, sheep-like followers of the State. Since they would be only incompletely developed, they would be only half-alive.

It might be said that no one is contemplating such monstrous measures. Even Communist Russia did not go so far as to impose a "communism of children," even though it did almost everything else to eliminate freedom. The point is, however, that this is the logical goal of the Statists in education. The issue which has been joined in the past and in the present is: shall there be a free society with parental control, or a despotism with State control? We shall see the logical development of the idea of State encroachment and control. America, for example, began, for the most part, with a system of either completely private or with philanthropic schools. Then, in the nineteenth century, the concept of public education changed subtly, until everybody was urged to go to the public school, and private schools were accused of being divisive. Finally, the State imposed compulsory education on the people, either forcing children to go to public schools or else setting up arbitrary standards for private schools. Parental instruction was frowned on. Thus, the State has been warring with parents for control over their children.

Not only has there been a trend toward increased State control, but the effects of this have been worsened by the very system of equality before the law that applies in political life. There has been the growth of a passion for equality in general. The result has been a tendency to regard every child as equal to every other child, as deserving equal treatment, and to impose complete uniformity in the classroom. Formerly, this had tended to be set at the average level of the class; but this being frustrating to the dullest (who, however, must be kept at the same level as the others, in the name of equality and democracy), the teaching tends more and more to be set at the lowest levels.

We shall see that since the State began to control education, its evident tendency has been more and more to act in such a manner as to promote repression and hindrance of education, rather than the true development of the individual. Its tendency has been for compulsion, for enforced equality at the lowest level, for the watering down of the subject and even the abandonment of all formal teaching, for the inculcation of obedience to the State and to the "group," rather than the development of self-independence, for the deprecation of intellectual subjects. And finally, it is the drive of the State and its minions for power that explains the "modern education" creed of "education of the whole child" and making the school a "slice of life," where the individual plays, adjusts to the group, etc. The effect of this, as well as all the other measures, is to repress any tendency for the development of reasoning powers and individual independence; to try to usurp in various ways the "educational" function (apart from formal instruction) of the home and friends, and to try to mold the "whole child" in the desired paths. Thus, "modern education" has abandoned the school functions of formal instruction in favor of molding the total personality both to enforce equality of learning at the level of the least educable, and to usurp the general educational role of home and other influences as much as possible. Since no one will accept outright State "communization" of children, even in Communist Russia, it is obvious that State control has to be achieved more silently and subtly.

For anyone who is interested in the dignity of human life, in the progress and development of the individual in a free society, the choice between parental and State control over the children is clear.

Is there, then, to be no State interference whatever in the relations between parent and child? Suppose that the parents aggress upon and mutilate the child? Are we to permit this? If not, where are we to draw the line? The line can be simply drawn. The State can adhere strictly to the function of defending everyone from the aggressive violence of everyone else. This will include children as well as adults, since children are potential adults and future freemen. Simple failure to "educate," or rather, instruct, is no grounds whatever for interference. The difference between these cases was succinctly put by Herbert Spencer:

> No cause for such [state] interposition can be shown until the children's rights have been violated, and that their rights are not violated by a neglect of their education [actually, instruction]. For...what we call rights are merely arbitrary subdivisions of the general liberty to exercise the faculties; and that only can be called an infringement of rights which actually diminishes this liberty—cuts off a previously existing power to pursue the objects of desire. Now the parent who is careless of a child's education does not do this. The liberty to exercise faculties is left intact. Omitting instruction in no way takes from a child's freedom to do whatsoever it wills in the best way it can, and this freedom is all that equity demands. Every aggression, be it remembered—every infraction of rights—is necessarily *active*; whilst every neglect, carelessness, omission, is as necessarily passive. Consequently, however wrong the non-performance of a parental duty may be...it does not amount to a breach of the law of equal freedom and cannot therefore be taken cognizance of by the state.[5]

## Children's Associations

Another powerful argument against compulsory education, one which is generally overlooked, is that, if instruction is compulsory, and the parent cannot afford to send his children to a private school or tutor, and is prevented from instructing the children himself, he must send his child to a public school. In the public school will be most of the others who would not be there were it not for the universal compulsory law. This includes subnormal, uneducable children, and various types of juvenile delinquents

---

[5]Herbert Spencer, *Social Statics: The Conditions Essential to Human Happiness Specified, and the First of Them Developed* (New York: Robert Schalkenbach Foundation, 1970), p. 294. Or as another writer expressed it, with regard to a parent and other members of the society: "his associates may not compel him to provide for his child, though they may forcibly prevent him from aggressing upon it. They may prevent acts; they may not compel the performance of actions." Clara Dixon Davidson, "Relations Between Parents and Children," *Liberty*, September 3, 1892.

and hoodlums. Whereas the parent would prefer not to send the child to formal schooling, rather than to compel him to associate with these vicious types, the State forces him to do so, with incalculably evil consequences to innocent children. Removed for part of the day from the care and supervision of the parent, the child is compelled to associate with vicious companions, and might even be influenced by them to join juvenile gangs, adopt drug addiction, etc.

These are not exaggerated evils, as any reader of the current press knows, but, true to the common hatred of individual superiority and distinction, the passion for leveling an enforced equality proclaims: this is good; let every child be forced to learn about "life" and be forced to associate with the lowest types of humanity. The envy and hatred toward the potentially better and superior child is apparent in this position, and underlies the argument for enforced equality and consequent suppression of superior individuality.

## Compulsory vs. Free Education

The Reverend George Harris described the effects of compulsory education in imposing uniformity and enforced equality (soon after the establishment of compulsion):

> Education is already so generally provided in America and other countries [1897], that, without forecasting imaginary conditions, there is no difficulty in seeing how much equality is given by that opportunity.... The same amount of time is given to all; the same courses are prescribed for all; the same teachers are appointed to all. The opportunity is not merely open; it is forced upon all. Even under a socialistic program it is difficult to imagine any arrangement for providing the education which all are supposed to need more nearly equal than the existing system of public schools. Even Mr. Bellamy [a prominent totalitarian socialist of the day] finds schools in the year 2000 AD modeled after those of the nineteenth century. All things are changed except the schools.... Behind fifty desks exactly alike fifty boys and girls are seated to recite a lesson prescribed to all.... But the algebra is not an opportunity for the boy who has no turn for mathematics.... Indeed, the more nearly equal the opportunity outwardly, the more unequal it is really. When the same instruction for the same number of hours a day by the same teachers is provided for fifty boys and girls, the

majority have almost no opportunity at all. The bright scholars are held back...the dull scholars are unable to keep up...average scholars are discouraged because the brighter pupils accomplish their tasks so easily.[6]

In the 1940s, the English writer and critic Herbert Read emphasized the diversity of man by pointing out the "psychological" objection to a compulsory "national system of education":

Mankind is naturally differentiated into many types, and to press all these types into the same mold must inevitably lead to distortions and repressions. Schools should be of many kinds, following different methods and catering for different dispositions. It might be argued that even a totalitarian state must recognize this principle but the truth is that differentiation is an organic process, the spontaneous and roving associations of individuals for particular purposes. To divide and segregate is not the same as to join and aggregate. It is just the opposite process. The whole structure of education as the natural process we have envisaged, falls to pieces if we attempt to make that structure...artificial.[7]

The great philosopher Herbert Spencer pointed out the despotism inherent in compulsory education:

For what is meant by saying that a government ought to educate the people? Why should they be educated? What is the education for? Clearly, to fit the people for social life—to make them good citizens. And who is to say what are good citizens? The government: there is no other judge. And who is to say how these good citizens may be made? The government: there is no other judge. Hence the proposition is convertible into this—a government ought to mold children into good citizens.... It must first form for itself a definite conception of a pattern citizen; and, having done this, must elaborate such system of discipline as seems best calculated to produce citizens after that pattern. This system of discipline it is bound to enforce to the uttermost. For if it does otherwise, it allows men to become different from what in its judgment they should become, and therefore fails in that duty it is charged to fulfill.[8]

---

[6]Harris, *Inequality and Progress*, pp. 42–43.

[7]Herbert Read, *The Education of Free Men* (London: Freedom Press, 1944), pp. 27–28.

[8]Spencer, *Social Statics*, p. 297.

Mrs. Isabel Paterson brilliantly sums up the tyranny of compulsory state education, and the superiority of free choice of private
education:

> political control is...by its nature, bound to legislate
> against statements of both facts and opinion, in prescrib-
> ing a school curriculum, in the long run. The most exact
> and demonstrable scientific knowledge will certainly be
> objectionable to political authority at some point,
> because it will expose the folly of such authority, and its
> vicious effects. Nobody would be permitted to show the
> nonsensical absurdity of "dialectical materialism" in
> Russia, by logical examination...and if the political
> authority is deemed competent to control education, that
> must be the outcome in any country.
>
> Educational texts are necessarily selective, in subject
> matter, language, and point of view. Where teaching is
> conducted by private schools, there will be a consider-
> able variation in different schools; the parents must
> judge what they want their children taught, by the cur-
> riculum offered. Then each must strive for objective
> truth.... Nowhere will there be any inducement to teach
> the "supremacy of the state" as a compulsory philoso-
> phy. But every politically controlled educational system
> will inculcate the doctrine of state supremacy sooner or
> later, whether as the divine right of kings, or the "will of
> the people" in "democracy." Once that doctrine has been
> accepted, it becomes an almost superhuman task to
> break the stranglehold of the political power over the life
> of the citizen. It has had his body, property, and mind in
> its clutches from infancy. An octopus would sooner
> release its prey.
>
> A tax-supported, compulsory educational system is the
> complete model of the totalitarian state.[9]

Here we must add that, in the current system, the State has
found a way in the United States, to induce the private schools to
teach State supremacy without outlawing private schools, as in
some other countries.

By enforcing certification for minimum standards, the State
effectively, though subtly, dominates the private schools and
makes them, in effect, extensions of the public school system. Only
removal of compulsory schooling and enforced standards will free
the private schools and permit them to function in independence.

[9]Isabel Paterson, *The God of the Machine* (Caldwell, Idaho: Caxton Printers, 1943), pp.
271–72.

Mrs. Paterson deals succinctly with the problem of compulsory education and literacy:

> But would not some children remain illiterate? They might, as some do now, and as they did in the past. The United States has had one president who did not learn to read and write until after he was not only a grown man, but married and earning his own living. The truth is that in a free country anyone who remains illiterate might as well be left so; although simple literacy is not a sufficient education in itself, but the elementary key to an indispensable part of education in civilization. But that further education in civilization *cannot be obtained at all* under full political control of the schools. It is possible only to a certain frame of mind in which knowledge is pursued voluntarily.

And Mrs. Paterson answers teachers and educators who would tend to reply in epithets to her criticism:

> Do you think nobody would *willingly* entrust his children to you to pay you for teaching them? Why do you have to...collect your pupils by compulsion?[10]

One of the best ways of regarding the problem of compulsory education is to think of the almost exact analogy in the area of that other great educational medium—the newspaper. What would we think of a proposal for the government, Federal or State, to use the taxpayers' money to set up a nationwide chain of public newspapers, and compel all people, or all children, to read them? What would we think furthermore of the government's outlawing all other newspapers, or indeed outlawing all newspapers that do not come up to the "standards" of what a government commission thinks children ought to read? Such a proposal would be generally regarded with horror in America, and yet this is exactly the sort of regime that the government has established in the sphere of scholastic instruction.

Compulsory public presses would be considered an invasion of the basic freedom of the press; yet is not scholastic freedom at least as important as press freedom? Aren't both vital media for public information and education, for free inquiry and the search for truth? It is clear that the suppression of free instruction should be

[10]Ibid, pp. 273 and 274; emphasis in original.

regarded with even greater horror than suppression of free press, since here the unformed minds of children are involved.

# Compulsory Education in Europe

T he record of the development of compulsory education is a record of State usurpation of parental control over children on behalf of its own; an imposition of uniformity and equality to repress individual growth; and the development of techniques to hinder the growth of reasoning power and independent thought among the children.

## Origins

We need not linger long over the status of education in ancient Greece and Rome. In Athens, the original practice of compulsory state education later gave way to a voluntary system. In Sparta, on the other hand, an ancient model for modern totalitarianism, the State was organized as one vast military camp, and the children were seized by the State and educated in barracks to the ideal of State obedience. Sparta realized the full logical conclusion of the compulsory system; absolute State control over the "whole child"; uniformity and education in passive obedience to State orders. The most important consequence of this system was that it provided the ideal for Plato, who made this educational system the basis of his ideal State, as set forth in the *Republic* and the *Laws*. Plato's "Utopia" was the first model for later despotisms—compulsory education and obedience were stressed, there was "communism" of children among the elite "guardians" who also had no private property, and lying was considered a proper instrument for the State to use in its indoctrination of the people.

In the Middle Ages, the problem of compulsory state education did not present itself in Europe. Instruction was carried on in church schools and universities, in private schools, and in private guild schools for occupational training. The first modern movement for compulsory state education stemmed directly from the Reformation. A prime force was Martin Luther. Luther repeatedly called for communities to establish public schools and to make attendance in them compulsory. In his famous letter to the German rulers in 1524, Luther used Statist premises to reach Statist conclusions:

> Dear rulers...I maintain that the civil authorities are under obligation to compel the people to send their children to school.... If the government can compel such citizens as are fit for military service to bear spear and rifle, to mount ramparts, and perform other martial duties in time of war, how much more has it a right to compel the people to send their children to school, because in this case we are warring with the devil, whose object it is secretly to exhaust our cities and principalities of their strong men.[1]

In this spiritual warfare, Luther of course was not speaking idly of the "devil" and the war against it. To him the war was a very real one.

As a result of Luther's urgings, the German state of Gotha founded the first modern public schools in 1524, and Thurungia followed in 1527. Luther himself founded the Saxony School Plan, which later became, in essence, the state education system for most of the Protestant States of Germany. This plan was put into effect first in Saxony in 1528, through an edict drawn up by Luther's important disciple Melanchthon, setting up state schools in every town and village. The first compulsory state system in the modern world was established in 1559 by Duke Christopher, Elector of Wurtemburg. Attendance was compulsory, attendance records were kept and fines were levied on truants. Other German states soon followed this example.

What was the spirit behind Luther's call for compulsory state education? A common view is that it reflected the Reformers' democratic spirit and the desire to have everyone read the Bible, the presumption being that they wished to encourage each one to interpret the Bible for himself.[2] The truth is quite otherwise. The

---

[1]Quoted in John William Perrin, *The History of Compulsory Education in New England,* 1896.

[2]For example, cf. Lawrence A. Cremin, *The American Common School: An Historic Conception* (New York: Teachers College, Columbia University, 1951), p. 84.

Reformers advocated compulsory education for all as a means of inculcating the entire population with their particular religious views, as an indispensable aid in effective "war with the devil" and the devil's agents. For Luther, these agents constituted a numerous legion: not only Jews, Catholics, and infidels, but also all other Protestant sects. Luther's political ideal was an absolute State guided by Lutheran principles and ministers. The fundamental principle was that the Bible, as interpreted by Luther, was the sole guide in all things. He argued that the Mosaic code awarded to false prophets the death penalty, and that it is the duty of the State to carry out the will of God. The State's duty is to force those whom the Lutheran Church excommunicates to be converted back into the fold. There is no salvation outside the Lutheran Church, and it is not only the duty of the State to compel all to be Lutherans, but its sole object. As the great historian Lord Acton stated of Luther:

> The defense of religion became...not only the duty of the civil power, but the object of its institution. Its business was solely the coercion of those who were out of the [Lutheran] Church.[3]

Luther stressed the theory of passive obedience, according to which no motives or provocation can justify a revolt against the State. In 1530, he declared: "It was the duty of a Christian to suffer wrong, and no breach of oath or of duty could deprive the Emperor of his right to the unconditional obedience of his subjects." In this way, he hoped to induce the princes to adopt and compel Lutheranism in their domains. Luther was expressly adamant that the State power be used with utmost severity against people who refused to be converted to Lutheranism. He required that all crimes should be punished with the utmost cruelty. The chief object of this severity was to be, of course, against the chief crime, refusal to adopt Lutheranism. The State must exterminate error, and could not tolerate heresy or heretics, "for no secular prince can permit his subjects to be divided by the preaching of opposite doctrines."

In sum: "Heretics are not to be disputed with, but to be condemned unheard, and whilst they perish by fire."

Such was the goal of the initial force behind the first compulsory state school system in the Western world, and such was the

---

[3]Cf. John, Lord Acton, "The Protestant Theory of Persecution" in his *Essays on Freedom and Power* (Glencoe, Ill.: The Free Press, 1948), pp. 88–127.

spirit that was to animate the system. No less ardent a despot was Melanchthon, Luther's principal aid in the drive for compulsory state schools in Germany.

Melanchthon taught firmly that all sects must be put down with the sword, and that any individual who originated new religious opinions should be punished with death. This punishment must be levied against any difference, however slight, in Protestant teachings. All others than Lutherans—Catholics, Anabaptists, Servetians, Zwinglians, etc., were to be persecuted with the utmost zeal.

The Lutheran influence on the political and educational life of the West, and particularly Germany, has been enormous. He was the first advocate of compulsory schooling, and his plans were the pattern for the first German schools. Furthermore, he inculcated Lutherans with the ideals of obedience to the State and persecution of all dissenters. As Acton states, he "impressed on his party that character of political dependence, and that habit of passive obedience to the State, which it has ever since retained."[4] A succinct estimate of Luther's influence on politics and compulsory education by an admirer follows:

> The permanent and positive value of Luther's pronouncement of 1524 lies not so much in its direct effects as in the hallowed associations which it established for Protestant Germany between the national religion and the educational duties of the individual and the state. Thus, doubtless, was created that healthy public opinion which rendered the principle of compulsory school attendance easy of acceptance in Prussia at a much later date than in England.[5]

Aside from Luther, the other leading influence toward the establishment of compulsory education in the modern world was the other great Reformer, John Calvin. Calvin went to Geneva in 1536, while the town was successfully revolting against the Duke of Savoy and the Catholic Church, and was appointed chief pastor and ruler of the city, which position he held until 1564. In Geneva, Calvin established a number of public schools, at which attendance was compulsory. What was the spirit that animated Calvin's

[4]Ibid., p. 94.

[5]A.E. Twentyman, "Education; Germany," *Encyclopedia Britannica*, 14th ed., vol. 7, pp. 999–1000.

establishment of the State school system? The spirit was the inculcation of the message of Calvinism, and obedience to the theocratic despotism which he had established. Calvin combined within himself political dictator and religious teacher. To Calvin, nothing mattered, no liberty or right was important, except his doctrine and its supremacy. Calvin's doctrine held that the support of Calvinism is the end and object of the State, and that this involves maintaining purity of doctrine and strict austerity in the behavior of the people. Only a small minority on earth are the "elect" (chief of whom is Calvin), and the rest are a mass of sinners who must be coerced by the sword, with the conquerors imposing Calvinist faith on the subjects. He did not favor killing all heretics. Catholics and Jews would be allowed to live, but all Protestants other than Calvinists must be killed. In some cases, however, he changed his position and advocated the severest punishment for Catholics as well.

Calvin, too, was adamant in asserting the duty of obedience to rulers regardless of their form of government. Government has divine sanction, and as long as it was Calvinist, it could pursue any course without deserving protest. Not only must all heretics be killed, but the same punishment should be meted out to those who deny the justice of such punishment. Calvin's leading disciples, such as Beza, were at least as ardent in promoting the extermination of heretics.

Calvin's influence on the Western world was wider than Luther's because, with diligent propaganda efforts, he made Geneva the European center for the widespread diffusion of his principles. Men from all over Europe came to study at Calvin's Schools and read his tracts, and the result was Calvinist influence throughout Europe.

As the Calvinists became important throughout Europe, they agitated for the establishment of compulsory state schools.[6] In 1560, the French Calvinists, the Huguenots, sent a memorandum to the king, requesting the establishment of universal compulsory education, but were turned down. In 1571, however, Queen Jeanne d'Albret, of the Estates of Navarre, under Calvinist influence, made primary education compulsory throughout that part of France. Calvinist Holland established compulsory public schools in 1609.

[6]Cf. Perrin, *The History of Compulsory Education in New England.*

John Knox, who conquered Scotland for his Presbyterian Church, was a Calvinist, although he had arrived at many of the principles independently. He established the Church along Calvinist lines, and proclaimed the death penalty for Catholics. Knox attempted to establish universal compulsory education in Scotland in the 1560s, but failed in the attempt. He advocated it in his *Book of Discipline*, which called for public schools in every Scottish town.

One of the most far-reaching effects of the Calvinist tradition is its influence on American educational history. Calvinist influence was strong among the English Puritans, and it was the Puritan influence that inaugurated public schools and compulsory education in New England, from whence it finally conquered the whole United States. The history of American compulsory education will be treated in the next section.

## Prussia

It is hardly coincidence that the most notoriously despotic State in Europe—Prussia—was the first to have a national system of compulsory education, nor that the original inspiration, as we have seen, was Luther and his doctrine of obedience to State absolutism. As Mr. Twentyman put it: "State interference in education was almost coincident with the rise of the Prussian state."

German education, as well as most of its other institutions and civilization, was completely disrupted by the Thirty Years Wars, in the first half of the seventeenth century. At the close of the conflict, however, the various state governments moved to make attendance of children at school compulsory upon penalty of fine and imprisonment of the children. The first step was taken by Gotha in 1643, followed by such states as Heildesheim in 1663, Prussia in 1669, and Calemberg in 1681.[7]

The state of Prussia began to rise in power and dominance at the beginning of the eighteenth century led by its first king, Frederick William I. Frederick William believed fervently in paternal despotism, and in the virtues of monarchical absolutism. One of his first measures was to effect a huge increase in the Prussian army, founded on an iron discipline which became famous throughout Europe. In civil administration, King Frederick William forged the centralizing engine of the Civil Service, which grew into the famous autocratic Prussian bureaucracy. In the commercial

---

[7]Cf. Howard C. Barnard, *National Education in Europe* (New York, 1854).

world, the King imposed restrictions, regulations, and subsidies on trade and business.

It was King Frederick William I who inaugurated the Prussian compulsory school system, the first national system in Europe. In 1717, he ordered compulsory attendance of all children at the state schools, and, in later acts, he followed with the provision for the construction of more such schools. It is perhaps appropriate that the King's personal attitudes were quite in keeping with his ardent promotion of despotism and militarism. As Cailfon Hayes states: "He treated his kingdom as a schoolroom, and like a zealous schoolmaster, flogged his naughty subjects unmercifully."

These beginnings were carried forward by his son Frederick the Great, who vigorously reasserted the principle of compulsory attendance in the state schools, and established the flourishing national system, particularly in his *Landschulreglement* of 1763. What were the goals that animated Frederick the Great? Again, a fervent belief in absolute despotism, although this was supposed to be "enlightened." "The prince," he declared, "is to the nation he governs what the head is to the man; it is his duty to see, think, and act for the whole community." He was particularly fond of the army, spent public funds freely upon it, and inculcated especially constant drill and the strictest discipline.

Modern Prussian despotism emerged as a direct result of the disastrous defeat inflicted by Napoleon. In 1807, the Prussian nation began to reorganize and gird itself for future victories. Under King Frederick William III, the absolute State was greatly strengthened. His famous minister, von Stein, began by abolishing the semi-religious private schools, and placing all education directly under the Minister of the Interior. In 1810, the ministry decreed the necessity of State examination and certification of all teachers. In 1812, the school graduation examination was revived as a necessary requirement for the child's departure from the state school, and an elaborate system of bureaucrats to supervise the schools was established in the country and the towns. It is also interesting that it was this reorganized system that first began to promote the new teaching philosophy of Pestalozzi, who was one of the early propounders of "progressive education."

Hand in hand with the compulsory school system went a revival and great extension of the army, and in particular the institution of universal compulsory military service.

Frederick William III continued the reorganization after the wars, and strengthened the compulsory state school system in 1834 by making it necessary for young entrants into the learned professions, as well as all candidates for the Civil Service and for university students to pass the high-school graduation examinations. In this way the Prussian state had effective control over all the rising generations of scholars and other professionals.

We will see in detail below that this despotic Prussian system formed an inspiring model for the leading professional educationists in the United States, who ruled the public school systems here and were largely responsible for its extension. For example, Calvin E. Stowe, one of the prominent American educators of the day, wrote a report on the Prussian system and praised it as worthy of imitation here.[8] Stowe lauded Prussia; although under the absolute monarchy of Frederick William III, it was the "best-educated" country in the world. Not only were there public schools in the elementary and higher grades, for pre-university and pre-business students, but also 1,700 teachers' seminaries for the training of future state teachers. Furthermore, there were stringent laws obliging parents to send their children to the schools. Children must attend the schools between the ages of seven and fourteen, and no excuses were permitted except physical inability or absolute idiocy. Parents of truants were warned, and finally punished by fines, or by civil disabilities, and as a last resort, the child was taken from its parents and educated and reared by the local authorities. Religious instruction was given in the schools in accordance with the religion of the locality, but the children were not obliged to attend these. However, it was compulsory for them to receive religious instruction in the home or from the church, in that case. Furthermore, the minister of education had to be a Protestant.

Private schools began to be permitted, but they were obliged to have the same standards of instruction as the state schools, and through these and the graduation examination requirements, the State was able to impose its control on all of the schools in the country.

Stowe felt that the Prussian methods of securing universality and uniformity of attendance were admirable. Another principle that he admired was that the Prussian State thereby imposed uniformity of

[8]Calvin E. Stowe, *The Prussian System of Public Instruction and Its Applicability to the United States* (Cincinnati, 1836).

language. Stowe asserted that the parents had no right to deprive their children of the unifying influence of the national language, "thus depriving them of the power of doing all the service to the State which they are capable of rendering."

The system of compulsory state education has been used as a terrible weapon in the hands of governments to impose certain languages and to destroy the languages of various national and linguistic groups within their borders. This was a particular problem in central and eastern Europe. The ruling State imposes its official language and culture on subject peoples with languages and cultures of their own, and the result has been incalculable bitterness. If the education were voluntary, such a problem would not have arisen. The importance of this aspect of compulsory education has been emphasized by economist Ludwig von Mises:

> The main tool of compulsory denationalization and assimilation is education....[I]n the linguistically mixed territories it turned into a dreadful weapon in the hands of governments determined to change the linguistic allegiance of their subjects. The philanthropists and pedagogues...who advocated public education did not foresee what waves of hatred and resentment would rise out of this institution.[9]

The Prussian educational system was extended to the rest of Germany upon the formation of Germany as a national state. Furthermore, a decree in 1872 strengthened the absolute control of the State over the schools against any possible incursions by the Catholic Church. The spirit that animated the German compulsory State was well expressed in a laudatory work:

> The prime fundamental of German education is that it is based on a national principle. Culture is the great capital of the German nation.... A fundamental feature of German education: Education to the State, education for the State, education by the State. The Volkschule is a direct result of a national principle aimed at national unity. The State is the supreme end in view.[10]

Another indication of the course that was set in the earliest and most eminent of the compulsory school systems, Prussia and

[9]Ludwig von Mises, *Omnipotent Government: The Rise of the Total State and Total War* (Spring Hills, Penn.: [1944] Libertarian Press, 1985), pp. 82–83.

[10]Franz de Hovre, *German and English Education, A Comparative Study* (London: Constable, 1917).

Germany, is revealed in a book of essays by leading German professors, setting forth the official German position in the first World War.[11] In this work, Ernst Troeltsch characterized Germany as being essentially a militaristic nation, greatly devoted to the army and to the monarchy. As for education:

> The school organization parallels that of the army, the public school corresponds to the popular army. The latter as well as the former was called into being during the first great rise of the coming German state in opposition to Napoleon. When Fichte considered the ways and means of resurrecting the German state, while the country was groaning under the Napoleonic yoke, he advised the infusion of German culture into the mass of the people, through the creation of national primary schools along the lines laid down by Pestalozzi. The program was actually adopted by the different German states, and developed during the last century into a comprehensive school system.... This has become the real formative factor of the German spirit. There is in this school system a Democratic and State–Socialist element such as Fichte intended.[12]

## France

Universal compulsory education, like compulsory military service, was ushered into France by the French Revolution. The revolutionary Constitution of 1791 decreed compulsory primary instruction for all. The Government could not do much to put these principles into effect at first, but it tried its best. In 1793, the Convention prescribed that the French language be the sole language of the "republic, one and indivisible." Little was done until the advent of Napoleon, who established a comprehensive state education. All schools, whether public or nominally private, were subject to the strict control of the national government. Dominating the entire system was the "University of France," which was established to insure uniformity and control throughout the entire French educational system. Its chief officials were appointed by Napoleon, and no one could open a new school or teach in public unless he was licensed by the official university. Thus, in this law of 1806, Napoleon acted to secure a monopoly of teaching to the

---

[11]*Modern Germany, In Relation to the Great War*, W. W. Whitlock, trans. (New York, 1916).

[12]Ernest Troeltsch, "The Spirit of German Kultur," *Modern Germany*, pp. 72–73. Also see Alexander H. Clay, *Compulsory Continuation Schools in Germany* (London, 1910).

State. The teaching staff of the public schools were to be routed through a normal school operated by the State. All these schools were directed to take as the basis of their teaching the principles of loyalty to the head of the State, and obedience to the statutes of the university. Due to lack of funds, the system of public schools could not then be imposed on all. By the end of the Napoleonic era, slightly less than half of French children attended public schools, the rest largely in Catholic schools. The private schools, however, were now under the regulation of the State and were obliged to teach patriotism on behalf of the rulers.

With the Restoration, the Napoleonic system was largely dismantled and education in France became predominantly a Catholic Church affair. After the revolution of 1830, however, Minister Guizot began to renew State power in his act of 1833. Attendance was not made compulsory, and the private schools were left intact, except for the significant requirement that all educational institutions must teach "internal and social peace." Complete liberty for private schools was restored, however, by the Falloux Law, passed in 1850 by Louis Napoleon.

With the exception, then, of the Revolutionary and Napoleonic periods, French education remained free until the latter part of the nineteenth century. Just as Prussian compulsion and absolutism had received a great impetus from the defeat at the hands of Napoleon, so did French compulsion and dictation receive its inspiration from the victory of Prussia in 1871. The Prussian victories were considered the victories of the Prussian army and the Prussian schoolmaster, and France, driven by the desire for revenge (*revanche*), set about to Prussianize its own institutions. In acts of 1882 and 1889, it inaugurated universal military conscription on the Prussian model.

Leader in the new policy was Minister Jules Ferry. Ferry was the main champion of a new policy of aggressive imperialism and colonial conquest. Aggressions were carried on in North Africa, in lower Africa, and in Indochina.

Demands for compulsory education arose from the goal of military *revanche*. As a leading politician Gambetta put it: "the Prussian schoolmaster had won the last war, and the French schoolmaster must win the next." To this end, a clamor arose for extension of the school system to every French child, for training in citizenship. Also, there were demands for compulsory education so that every

French child would be inoculated in republicanism and immune to the lures of monarchical restoration. As a result, Ferry, in a series of laws in 1881 and 1882, made French education compulsory. Private schools were nominally left free, but actually were greatly restricted by the compulsory dissolution of the Jesuit Order and its expulsion from France. Many of the private schools in France had been run by the Jesuits. Moreover, the laws abolished many monastic orders which had not been formally "authorized" by the State, and forbade their members to conduct schools. Attendance at some school was compulsory for all children between six and thirteen years of age.

The effect of the new regime was to dominate the private schools completely, since those that were not affected by the anti-Catholic laws had to subsist under the decree that "private schools cannot be established without a license from the minister, and can be shut up by a simple ministerial order."[13] Private secondary schools were severely crippled by the Walleck-Rousseau and Combes acts of 1901 and 1904, which suppressed all private religious secondary schools in France.

## Other Countries

The story of compulsory education in the other countries of Europe is quite similar, with the added element of compulsory languages in most of them. The Austro-Hungarian Empire strove for a uniform, centralized absolute monarchy, with the language to be solely German, while the Hungarian segment of the empire attempted to "Magyarize" its minority nationalities and abolish all languages except Hungarian within its borders. Spain has used its compulsory school acts to suppress the Catalan language and to impose Castilian. Switzerland has a system of compulsory schooling ingrained into its Constitution. In general, every country in Europe had established compulsory education by 1900, with the exception of Belgium, which followed by 1920.[14]

---

[13]Herbert Spencer, *Social Statics* (New York: Robert Schalkenbach Foundation, 1970), p. 297.

[14]For a detailed tabulation of the compulsory education laws in each country of Europe at the turn of the century, see *London Board of Education, Statement as to the Age at Which Compulsory Education Begins in Certain Foreign Countries* (London, 1906). The vast majority had compulsory schooling from the ages of 6 or 7 until 14.

To Herbert Spencer, China carried out the idea of compulsory education to its logical conclusion:

> There the government publishes a list of works which may be read; and considering obedience the supreme virtue, authorizes such only as are friendly to despotism. Fearing the unsettling effects of innovation, it allows nothing to be taught but what proceeds from itself. To the end of producing pattern citizens, it exerts a stringent discipline over all conduct. There are "rules for sitting, standing, walking, talking, and bowing, laid down with the greatest precision."[15]

The Imperial Japanese system of compulsory state education is worth noting carefully, because of the many similarities which it displays with modern "progressive" education. As Lafcadio Hearn observed:

> The object has never been to train the individual for independent action, but to train him for cooperative action.... Constraint among us begins with childhood, and gradually relaxes [which would be the best for the child as his reasoning powers develop and he could be allowed more freedom and less guidance]; constraint in Far Eastern training begins later, and thereafter gradually tightens.... Not merely up to the age of school life, but considerably beyond it, a Japanese child enjoys a degree of liberty far greater than is allowed to Occidental children.... The child is permitted to do as he pleases.... At school, the discipline begins...but there is no punishment beyond public admonition. *Whatever restraint exists is chiefly exerted on the child by the common opinion of his class*; and a skillful teacher is able to direct that opinion.... The ruling power is always the class sentiment.... It is always the rule of the many over the one; and the power is formidable.

The spirit inculcated is always the sacrifice of the individual to the community, and a crushing of any individual independence. In adult life, any deviation from the minutiae of state regulation was instantly and severely punished.[16]

---

[15]Spencer, op. cit., pp 297–98.

[16]Quotations from Lafcadio Hearn, *Japan: An Interpretation*, (New York: Macmillan, 1894), in Isabel Paterson, *The God of the Machine*, (Caldwell, Idaho: Caxton Printers, 1964), pp. 265–66.

## England

The tradition of voluntarism was at its strongest in England. So strong was it that, not only was there no compulsory education in England until the late nineteenth century, but there was not even a public school system. Before the 1830s, the State did not interfere in education at all. After 1833, the State began to make ever-increasing grants to promote indirectly the education of the poor in private schools. This was strictly philanthropic, and there was no trace of compulsion. Finally, compulsion was introduced into English education in the famous Education Act of 1870. This act permitted County boards to make attendance compulsory. London County immediately did so for children between five and thirteen, and other large towns followed suit. The rural counties, however, were reluctant to impose compulsory attendance. By 1876, 50 percent of the school population was under compulsion in Britain, and 84 percent of the city children.[17] The Act of 1876 set up school attendance boards in those areas where there were no school boards, and attendance was compulsory in all of those remote areas, except where children lived more than two miles from school. Finally, the Act of 1880 compelled all the county school boards to decree and enforce compulsory attendance. Thus, in a decade, compulsory education had conquered England.

The great legal historian A.V. Dicey analyzed this development in no uncertain terms as part of the movement toward collectivism:

> It means, in the first place, that A, who educates his children at his own expense, or has no children to educate is compelled to pay for the education of the children of S, who, though maybe having means to pay for it, prefers that the payment should come from the pockets of his neighbors. It tends, in the second place, as far as elementary education goes, to place the children of the rich and of the poor, of the provident and the improvident, on something like an equal footing. It aims, in short at the equalization of advantage.[18]

---

[17]Howard C. Barnard, *A Short History of English Education, 1760–1944* (London: University of London Press, 1947). Strictly, the first element of compulsion had been introduced in 1844, since some of the Factory Acts had required children to be educated before beginning to work.

[18]A.V. Dicey, *Lectures on the Relation between Law and Public Opinion in England During the Nineteenth Century* (New York: Macmillan, 1948), pp. 276–278.

The compulsory collectivist principle represented quite a clash with the individualist tradition in England. The notable Newcastle Commission in 1861 rejected the idea of compulsory education on the grounds of individualistic principle. Trenchant criticism of the compulsory state education plan as a capstone of growing State tyranny was leveled by Herbert Spencer[19] and by the eminent historian and jurist Sir Henry Maine.[20] In recent years, Arnold Toynbee has pointed out how compulsory state education stifles independent thought.[21]

The movement for compulsory education in England and Europe in the late nineteenth century was bolstered by trade unionists who wanted more popular education, and upper classes who wished to instruct the masses in the proper exercise of their voting rights. Each group in society characteristically wished to add to State power with their particular policies hopefully prevailing in the use of that power.

The change of opinion in England was particularly swift on this issue. When Dicey wrote in 1905, he declared that scarcely anyone could be found to attack compulsory education. Yet, when John Stuart Mill wrote his *On Liberty* in 1859, he declared that scarcely anyone could be found who would not strenuously oppose compulsory education. Mill, curiously enough, supported compulsory education, but opposed the erection of any public schools, and, indeed, it turned out that in England, compulsion came before public schools in many areas. Mill, however, at least recognized that compulsory state schooling would abolish individuality on behalf of State uniformity, and would naturally make for obedience to the State.

Mill's argument for compelling education was successfully refuted by Spencer in *Social Statics*. Mill had asserted that in education the consumer does not know what is best for him, and that therefore the government is justified in intervening. Yet, as Spencer points out, this has been the excuse for almost every exercise in State tyranny. The only proper test of worth is the judgment of the

---

[19]In *The Man Versus the State* (Caldwell, Idaho: Caxton Printers, 1946).

[20]Sir Henry Maine, *Popular Government* (Indianapolis, Ind.: Liberty Classics, [1885] 1976).

[21]Arnold J. Toynbee, *A Study of History*, 10 vols. (New York: Oxford University Press, 1962), vol. 4, pp. 196–97.

consumer who actually uses the product. And the State's judgment is bound to be governed by its own despotic interests.

Another common argument in England for compulsory education was also prevalent in the United States. This was Macauley's argument—education would eliminate crime, and since it is the duty of the State to repress crime the State should institute compulsory education. Spencer showed the speciousness of this argument, demonstrating that crime has little to do with education. This has become all too evident now, a glance at our growing juvenile delinquency rate in compulsorily educated America is proof enough of that. Spencer investigated the statistics of his day, and demonstrated that there was no correlation between ill-educated areas and criminal areas; indeed, in many cases, the correlation was the reverse—the more education, the more crime.

### Fascism, Nazism, and Communism

It is a grave and unanswerable indictment of compulsory state education that these modern totalitarianisms were eager to institute compulsory state schooling in their regimes. Indeed, the indoctrination of the youth in their schools was one of the chief mainstays of these slave-states. As a matter of fact, the chief difference between the twentieth-century horrors and the older despotisms is that the present ones have had to rest on mass support more directly, and that therefore compulsory literacy and indoctrination have been crucial. The compulsory state system already developed was grist for the totalitarian mill.[22] At the base of totalitarianism and compulsory education is the idea that children belong to the State rather than to their parents. One of the leading promoters of that idea in Europe was the famous Marquis de Sade, who insisted that children are the property of the State.

There is no need to dwell on education in Communist countries. Communist countries impose compulsory state schooling, and enforce rigid indoctrination of obedience to the rulers. The compulsory schooling is supplemented by State monopolies on other propaganda and educational fields.

Similarly, National Socialist education subordinated the individual to the State and enforced obedience. Education belonged

---

[22]See Erik von Kuehnelt-Leddihn, *Liberty or Equality* (Caldwell, Idaho: Caxton Printers, 1952), pp. 63–64.

exclusively to the National Socialist state for indoctrination in its principles.

A similar use of state schools and indoctrination for obedience to the absolute State was employed in Fascist Italy. Italy is particularly interesting for the activities of the first Fascist Minister of Education Giovanni Gentile. For in lax old Italy, education had stressed the intellectual development of the individual child and his learning of subjects. Gentile's Fascist regime instituted the methods of modern "progressive education." He introduced and emphasized manual work, singing, drawing, and games. Attendance was enforced by fines. Significantly, Gentile taught that "education must be achieved through experience, it must be achieved through action."[23] The children were free to learn through their own experiences, of course "within the limits necessary for development of culture. "Curricula were therefore not prescribed, but children were free to do as they wanted, with the only emphasis of study placed on "the study of heroes such as Mussolini as symbols of the national spirit."[24]

[23]The similarity to John Dewey's dictum of "learning by doing" is obvious. This will be discussed below. See Franklin L. Burdette, "Politics and Education," pp. 410–23, esp. 419, in *Twentieth Century Political Thought*, ed. J. Roucek (New York: Philosophical Library, 1946).

[24]See, among others, H.W. Schneider and S.B. Clough, *Making Fascists* (Chicago: University of Chicago Press, 1929); George F. Kneller, *The Educational Philosophy of National Socialism* (New Haven, Conn.: Yale University Press, 1941); Walter Lando, "Basic Principles of National Socialist Education," *Education for Dynamic Citizenship* (Philadelphia: University of Pennsylvania Press, 1937); Howard R. Marraro, *The New Education in Italy* (New York: S.F. Vauni, 1936); Albert P. Pinkevitch, *The New Education in the Soviet Republic* (New York: John Day Company, 1929). Also of interest is Edward H. Riesner, *Nationalism and Education Since 1789: A Social and Political History of Modern Education* (New York: Macmillan, 1922) for background.

# Compulsory Education
# in the United States

## The Development of Compulsory Education

Perhaps some people might feel that identification of compulsory education with tyranny could not be applicable to a free country such as the United States. On the contrary, the spirit and record of compulsory education in America point to very similar dangers.

In the majority of American colonies, education was in the English tradition, i.e., voluntary parental education, with the only public schools being those established for poor families free to make use of the facilities. This system originated in the Middle and in the Southern colonies. The crucial exception was New England, the sparkplug of the collectivist educational system in America. In contrast to the other colonies, New England was dominated by the Calvinist tradition, among the English Puritans who settled Massachusetts, and later the other New England colonies.[1] The ruthless and ascetic Puritans who founded the Massachusetts Bay Colony were eager to adopt the Calvinist plan of compulsory education in order to insure the creation of good Calvinists and the suppression of any possible dissent. Only a year after its first set of particular laws, the Massachusetts Bay Colony in 1642 enacted a compulsory literacy law for all children. Furthermore, whenever

---

[1]John William Perrin, *The History of Compulsory Education in New England*, 1896; Lawrence Cremin, *The American Common School, an Historic Conception* (Teachers College, New York, 1951); and Forest Chester Ensign, *Compulsory School Attendance and Child Labor* (Iowa City: Athens Press, 1921).

the state officials judged that the parents or guardians were unfit or unable to take care of the children properly, the state could seize the children and apprentice them to the state appointees, who would give them the required instruction.

This law of June 14, 1642, was notable, because it was the first establishment of compulsory education in the English-speaking world. It therefore deserves quoting in some detail:

> For as much as the good education of children is of sin-
> gular behoof and benefit to any commonwealth, and
> whereas many parents and masters are too indulgent
> and negligent of their duty of that kind, it is ordered that
> the selectmen of every town...shall have a vigilant eye
> over their neighbors, to see first that none shall suffer so
> much barbarism in any of their families, as not to
> endeavor to teach, by themselves or others, their chil-
> dren and apprentices.[2]

In 1647, the colony followed up this law with the establishment of public schools. The major stress in the compulsory education was laid on the teaching of Calvinist–Puritan principles.

It is significant that the slightly older and more religiously liberal Pilgrim colony of Plymouth did not set up a compulsory educational system. When the Plymouth colony was merged into the Massachusetts Bay, however, the latter's education laws prevailed.

What was the sort of government that set up the English-speaking world's first compulsory educational system, the future inspiration for the educational systems of the other states? The spirit of the government was Calvinist absolutism. Everyone in the colony was forced to attend a Congregational Church, although not everyone could qualify as a member. Only Church members, however, could vote in the state elections. The principles of this theocratic government were that of "order," with the superior and the inferior put in their proper place. The ministerial authority of the elders of the church was to prevail. In order to be admitted to church membership (and voting rights), the candidate had to be scrutinized by the elders of the church, who determined whether or not there was "something of God and Grace" in his soul, and therefore fit as a member. The great spiritual Puritan leader the Rev. John Cotton, however, declared that hypocrites who merely conform to the elders' rules without inner belief could still be

---

[2]Perrin, *The History of Compulsory Education in New England.*

members—provided that they were not idle in their occupations. It is interesting to note that the colony set up Harvard College in one of its first acts, in 1636, as a state college. The authorities declared that schools must depend on the magistrates, in order to prevent the corruption of sound doctrines.

Another leading Puritan minister and ruler the Rev. William Hubbard declared that "it is found by experience...that the greatest part of mankind are but as tools and instruments for others to work by, rather than any proper agents to effect anything of themselves." They are always sheep requiring a shepherd. The magistrates are the governing force, the "head" of society. The Rev. John Davenport advised the electors to choose good rulers, because it was imperative for them to submit to the ruler's authority.

> You must submit to their authority, and perform all duties to them whom you have chosen...whether they be good or bad, by virtue of their Relation between them and you.

Thus, formal democracy was early seen to be compatible with despotism of the rulers over the ruled.

The most important influence in shaping the Massachusetts Bay Colony was its first governor John Winthrop, who ruled the colony for twenty years from its inception in 1630. Winthrop believed that natural liberty is a "wild beast" which must be restrained by "God's ordinances." Correct civil liberty means being good "in a way of subjection to authority." Winthrop regarded any opposition to the policies of the governor, particularly when he was the governor, as positively seditious.

The governing of Massachusetts was fully in keeping with these principles. Heretics and assumed witches were persecuted and hounded, and Puritan austerity and strict conformity in almost all areas of life were enforced. Dissenters, like Roger Williams and Anne Hutchinson, had to leave the colony.

The Puritans soon spread out to other states, and Connecticut was governed in the same spirit. Rhode Island, however, was far more liberal, and it is no coincidence that Rhode Island was the exception in New England in the setting up of state school systems during the colonial period.

During the eighteenth century, the colonial religious severity gradually weakened its hold on the community. More sects arose and flourished. Massachusetts and Connecticut, however, enacted repressive laws against the Quakers, forbidding them also to establish schools. Furthermore, Connecticut, in a vain attempt to suppress the "New Light" movement, enacted a law in 1742 forbidding the New Lights from establishing any schools. Their reasons: that this "may tend to train youth in principles and practices, and introduce such disorders as may be of fatal consequences to the public peace and weal of this colony."[3]

Some of the motivation for the religious indoctrination and compulsory education in the colonial period was economic. Servants were particularly required to be instructed, as many of their masters believed that the servants were less prone to be independent and to "give trouble" when imbued with the catechism and the Puritan Bible.

Finally, the Revolutionary War disrupted the entire education system, and the independent states were ready to begin anew. The new States met the problem very much as they had done as colonies. Once again, Massachusetts led the way in establishing compulsory education, which her colonial laws had always provided. She took the unusual step of including in her State Constitution of 1780 a provision expressly granting authority to the legislature to enforce compulsory attendance at school. This authority was promptly exercised, and in 1789 school attendance was made compulsory in Massachusetts. Connecticut followed in 1805 with a law requiring all parents to educate their children.

Connecticut followed this compulsory literacy with a law in 1842 requiring all employed children under fifteen to attend school for three months during a year, thus adding a compulsory schooling to its general elementary compulsory education, or literacy, laws. Massachusetts's laws were lax on truants, however, and in 1845 Boston attempted to pass a bill against truancy of unemployed children, but lost on the ground that the rights of parents were threatened. The bill did pass in 1846, however. In 1850 Massachusetts authorized its towns to make provisions for habitual truants, and provided that they could be confined in prison. Finally in 1852, Massachusetts established the first comprehensive statewide, modern system of compulsory schooling in the United

---

[3]Merle E. Curti, *The Social Ideas of American Educators* (Paterson, N.J.: Pageant Books, 1959).

States. It provided that all children between eight and fourteen had to attend school at least thirteen weeks each year. Massachusetts, over the rest of the century, continued to extend and strengthen its compulsory education laws. In 1862, for example, it made jailing of habitual truant children mandatory, and extended school age to between ages seven and sixteen. In 1866, school attendance was made compulsory for six months during the year.

This is not the place for a discussion of the "battle for the public schools" that transformed the American educational system from 1800 to 1850. The goal of the proponents of the drive will be analyzed. But suffice it to say that, between 1825 and 1850, the propaganda work had been such that the non-New England states had changed from a system of no public schools, or only pauper schools, to the establishment of free schools available to all. Furthermore, the spirit of the schools had changed from philanthropy to the poor to something which all children were induced to attend. By 1850, every state had a network of free public schools.

In 1850, all the states had public schools, but only Massachusetts and Connecticut were imposing compulsion. The movement for compulsory schooling conquered all of America in the late nineteenth century. Massachusetts began the parade, and the other states all followed, mainly in the 1870s and 1880s. By 1900, almost every state was enforcing compulsory attendance.[4]

There seemed to have been little debate over the issue of compulsory schooling. We can only guess at the reason for this neglect of a fundamental issue, a neglect that is evident, furthermore, in every history of education. It may well be because the professional "educationists" knew that the issue might be a touchy one if the topic were unduly stressed in public debate. After citing some of the pro- and con-opinions on the compulsory–schooling laws, we will investigate the development of the "educationists" and their propaganda movements, since they were instrumental in establishing public schools and in ruling their operations to this day.

---

[4]For a list of the dates of the establishment of the compulsion laws in the states, cf. Edgar W. Knight, and Clifton L. Hall, *Readings in American Educations History* (New York: Appleton–Century, Crofts, 1951). For a detailed chart of the compulsory education laws in force in various states in 1905, see *Report of the Commissioner of Education for 1906*, chap. 28, "Compulsory Attendance and its Relation to the General Welfare of the Child" (Washington, D.C.: U.S. Government Printing Office, 1906).

## Arguments For and Against Compulsion in the United States

The individualist tradition on this matter was well presented in the early nineteenth century by Thomas Jefferson. Although an ardent advocate of public schools to aid the poor, Jefferson squarely rejected compulsion:

> It is better to tolerate the rare instance of a parent refusing to let his child be educated, than to shock the common feelings and ideas by the forcible transportation and education of the infant against the will of the father.[5]

Similarly, a fellow Virginian of that period warned against any transfer of the rights of the parents to the government, thereby jeopardizing the vital relation between parent and child.[6]

By the late nineteenth century, however, the individualist tradition had dwindled sharply. Typical in support of compulsory education was a report prepared by one of the professional educationist groups, the Public Education Association of Philadelphia in 1898.[7] It resolved that as long as there are ignorant or selfish parents, compulsion must be used in order to safeguard the child's rights. The report complained that the Pennsylvania Compulsory Education Law of 1895 did not take effect in the city of Philadelphia, and recommended that it do so. It indicated that one of the major forces for such laws came from the budding trade union movement.[8]

The report greatly praised the Prussian system and its compulsory attendance record. It praised Massachusetts and Prussia for their systems of only permitting schooling in private schools when they fulfilled the requirements imposed by the government school committee. It also lauded the fact that Massachusetts and New York had set up truant schools, and if parents refused to give permission for their truant child to be sent there, the courts could commit him to the institution.

The spirit of the professional educationists is indicated in some of the statements mentioned in this report. Thus, a Brooklyn educator

---

[5]Cf. Saul K. Padover, *Jefferson* (New York: Harcourt, Brace and Company, 1942), p. 169.

[6]"A Constituent," *Richmond (Va.) Enquirer*, January 1818.

[7]*Compulsory Education*, prepared for the Public Education Association of Philadelphia, 1898.

[8]Cf. Philip Curoe, *Educational Attitudes and Policies of Organized Labor in the United States* (New York: Teachers College, Columbia University, 1926).

criticized the existing system of discharging truant children on July 31 of each year, and advocated that the sentence be extended indefinitely until evidence of reform is shown, or until the child is past school age.

In other words, complete seizure and incarceration of young truants. A school superintendent of Newburgh, New York, suggested that children over fourteen who had not attended school, and who were therefore above the age limit for compulsion, should be forced to attend schools for manual training, music, and military drill.

Prussia was also the ideal for a prominent newspaper supporting compulsory education. The influential *New York Sun* declared that children must have education, and that they should be obliged to receive it from the State; it praised the universality of the compulsory education system in Prussia and other German states.[9]

In 1872, Secretary B.G. Northrup of the Connecticut State Board of Education felt it self-evident that the children had "sacred rights" to education, and that growing up in ignorance was a "crime." (We have seen in the first section that everyone, including the illiterate, attain knowledge and "education," even if not formally instructed.)

The leading educationist body, the National Education Association, resolved in its 1897 meeting in favor of state laws for compulsory attendance.[10]

Thus we see that the professional educationists were the major force, assisted by the trade unions, in imposing compulsory education in America.

There was a flurry of opposition to compulsory education in the early 1890s, but by that time the movement was on its way to a clear victory. Twice, in 1891 and 1893, Governor Pattison of Pennsylvania, a state with a tradition of freedom in education, vetoed compulsory education bills on the grounds that any interference with the personal liberty of the parents is un-American in principle. The law passed in 1895, however, when Governor Hasting

[9]*New York Sun,* 16 April 1867.

[10]*Journal of Proceedings and Addresses,* N.E.A., 1897, p. 196.

signed the bill with great reluctance.[11] In 1892, the Democratic
Party National Platform declared:

> We are opposed to state interference with parental rights
> and rights of conscience in the education of children as
> an infringement of the fundamental Democratic doctrine
> that the largest individual liberty consistent with the
> rights of others insures the highest type of American cit-
> izenship and the best government.[12]

## The Goals of Public Schooling: The Educationist Movement

It is important to consider the goals of the establishment of public schools, particularly since professional educators were the
prime force in both the establishment of free common schools and
of compulsory instruction. In the first place, the desire for public
schools by such quasi-libertarians as Thomas Jefferson and
Thomas Paine was based on a belief that republican government is
best suited for well-schooled citizens, and that the government
should make such institutions available for those too poor to
afford them privately.[13] Certainly, many of those who advocated
the establishment of public schools did it simply for this reason.

There were other and more dangerous goals, however, particularly among the educationists who were the main forces in the
drive, and who took control of the state boards of education and
teachers' training colleges which instructed the public school
teachers. As early as 1785, the Rev. Jeremy Belknap, preaching
before the New Hampshire General Court, advocated equal and
compulsory education for all, emphasizing that the children
belong to the State and not to their parents.[14] The influential Ben-
jamin Rush wanted general education in order to establish a uniform, homogeneous, and egalitarian nation.

The doctrine of obedience to the State was the prime goal of the
father of the public school system in North Carolina, Archibald D.

---

[11] Knight and Hall, *Readings in American Educational History.*

[12] Ibid.; and H.L. Mencken, *A New Dictionary of Quotations on Historical Principles from Ancient and Modern Sources* (New York: A.A. Knopf, 1942), pp. 333–34.

[13] Cremin, *The History of Compulsory Education in New England.*

[14] Hans Kohn, *The Idea of Nationalism: A Study in Its Origins and Background* (New York: Macmillan, 1934), p. 104.

Murphey. In 1816, Murphey planned a system of state schools as follows:

> all children will be taught in them...in these schools the precepts of morality and religion should be inculcated, and habits of subordination and obedience be formed.... The state, in the warmth of her solicitude for their welfare, must take charge of those children, and place them in school where their minds can be enlightened and their hearts can be trained to virtue.[15]

By the 1820s, their goals of compulsion and statism were already germinating over the country, and particularly flourishing in New England, although the individualist tradition was still strong. One factor that increased the power of New England in diffusing the collectivist idea in education was the enormous migration from that area. New Englanders swarmed south and west out of New England, and carried their zeal for public schooling and for State compulsion with them.

Into this atmosphere was injected the closest that the country had seen to Plato's idea, of full State communistic control over the children. This was the plan of two of the first socialists in America—Frances Wright and Robert Dale Owen. Owen was the son of one of the first British "Utopian" Socialists, and with Robert Owen, his father, had attempted an experiment in a voluntary-communist community in New Harmony, Indiana. Frances Wright was a Scotswoman who had also been at New Harmony, and with Owen, opened a newspaper called the *Free Enquirer*. Their main objective was to campaign for their compulsory education system. Wright and Owen outlined their scheme as follows:

> It is national, rational, republican education; free for all at the expense of all; conducted under the guardianship of the State, and for the honor, the happiness, the virtue, the salvation of the state.[16]

The major aim of the plan was that equality be implanted in the minds, the habits, the manners, and the feelings, so that eventually fortunes and conditions would be equalized. Instead of the intricate

---

[15]Archibald D. Murphey, *The Papers of Archibald D. Murphey*, 2 vols. (Raleigh, N.C.: E.M. Uzzell, 1914), pp. 53–54.

[16]Robert Dale Owen and Frances Wright, *Tracts on Republican Government and National Education* (London, 1847). Also, see Cremin, *The History of Compulsory Education in New England*.

apparatus of common schools, high schools, seminaries, etc., Wright and Owen advocated that the states simply organize a series of institutions for the "general reception" of all children living within that district. These establishments would be devoted to the complete rearing of the various age groups of children. The children would be forced to live at these places twenty-four hours a day. The parents would be allowed to visit their children from time to time. From the age of two every child would be under the care and guidance of the State.

> In these nurseries of a free nation, no inequality must be allowed to enter. Fed at a common board; clothed in a common garb...raised in the exercise of common duties... in the exercise of the same virtues, in the enjoyment of the same pleasures; in the study of the same nature; in pursuit of the same object...say! Would not such a race...work out the reform of society and perfect the free institutions of America?

Owen was quite insistent that the system not "embrace anything less than the whole people." The effect will be to "regenerate America in one generation. It will make but one class out of the many." Frances Wright revealed the aim of the system starkly, calling on the people to overthrow a moneyed aristocracy and priestly hierarchy. "The present is a war of class."

Thus, we see that a new element has been introduced into the old use of compulsory education on behalf of State absolutism. A second goal is absolute equality and uniformity, and a compulsory school system was seen by Owen and Wright to be ideally suited to this task. First, the habits and minds and feelings of all the children must be molded into absolute equality; and then the nation will be ripe for the final step of equalization of property and incomes by means of State coercion.

Why did Owen and Wright insist on seizing the children for twenty-four hours a day, from the age of two on, only releasing them when the school age was over at sixteen? As Owen declared:

> In republican schools, there must be no temptation to the growth of aristocratical prejudices. The pupils must learn to consider themselves as fellow citizens, as equals. Respect ought not to be paid to riches, or withheld from poverty. Yet, if the children from these state Schools are to go every evening, the one to his wealthy parent's soft carpeted drawing room, and the other to its poor father's

or widowed mother's comfortless cabin, will they return
the next day as friends and equals?

Likewise, differences in quality of clothing invoked feelings of
envy on the part of the poor and disdain by the rich—which
should be eliminated by forcing one uniform upon both. Throughout his plans there runs the hatred of human diversity, particularly
of the higher living standards of the rich as compared to the poor.
To effect his plan for thoroughgoing equalization by force, the
schools

> must receive the children, not for six hours a day, but
> altogether must feed them, clothe them, lodge them;
> must direct not their studies only, but their occupations
> and amusements and must care for them until their edu-
> cation is completed.

It might be asserted that the Owen–Wright plan is unimportant;
that it had purely crackpot significance and little influence. The
contrary is true. In the first place, the plan had a great deal of influence: certainly the ideas of promoting equality were dominant in
the thinking of the influential group of educationists that established and controlled the public schools of the nation during the
1830s and 1840s. Furthermore, the Owen plan pushes the whole
idea of compulsory state schooling to its logical conclusion—not
only by promoting State absolutism and absolute equality—to
which the system is admirably suited, but also because Owen recognized that he had to educate the "whole child" in order to mold
the coming generation sufficiently. Is it not probable that the "progressive" drive to educate the "whole child" aims to mold the
child's entire personality in lieu of the complete Owen–Wright
compulsory communist seizure, which no one in America would
accept?

The influence of the Owen–Wright plan is attested to by the fact
that a contemporary laudatory historian of the public-school
movement places it first in his story, and devotes considerable
space to it.[17] Cremin reports that a great many newspapers
reprinted Owen's essays on the plan, and approved them. Owen
began expounding his project in the late 1820s and continued on
until the late 1840s, when he wrote the elaborated plan with Miss
Wright. It had a considerable influence on workers' groups. It

---

[17]Cremin, op. cit, pp. 37 ff.

exerted a great influence on the widely noted report of a committee of Philadelphia workers in 1829 to report on education in Pennsylvania. The report called for equality, and equal education and proper training for all. And this and similar reports "had a considerable influence in preparing the way for the progressive legislation of the middle thirties."[18]

Shortly thereafter, there arose on the American scene a remarkable phenomenon: a closely-knit group of educationists. Cremin calls them "educational reformers" whose tireless propaganda was instrumental in pushing through public schools, who then came to control the schools through positions on the state boards of education, as superintendents, etc.; through the control of teachers' training institutions, and thereby of the teachers. This same grouping, under different names, continues to dominate primary and secondary education to this day, with their own tightly knit ideas and jargon. Most important, they have managed to impose their standards on state certification requirements for teachers, so that no one can teach in a public school who does not go through a course of teacher-training instruction run by the educationists. It was this same group that pushed through compulsory education, and advocated more and more "progressive" education, and therefore they deserve close scrutiny.

Some Americans pride themselves that their educational system can never be tyrannical, because it is not federally, but state, controlled. This makes very little difference, however. Not only does this still mean the government, whether state or Federal, but also the educationists, through national associations and journals, are almost completely coordinated. In actuality, therefore, the school systems are nationally and centrally controlled, and formal Federal control would only be the crowning step in the drive for national conformity and control.

Another important source of tyranny and absolutism in the school system is the fact that the teachers are under Civil Service. As a result, once a formal examination is passed—and this has little relation to actual teaching competence—and a little time elapses, the teacher is on the public payroll, and foisted on the children for the rest of his working life. The government bureaucracy has fostered Civil Service as an extraordinarily powerful tool of

[18] Ibid.

entrenchment and permanent domination. Tyranny by majority vote may be unpleasant enough, but at least if the rulers are subject to democratic checks, they have to please the majority of the voters. But government officials who cannot be voted out at the next election are not subject to any democratic check whatever. They are permanent tyrants. "Taking something out of politics" by putting it under Civil Service certainly does "increase the morale" of the bureaucracy. It elevates them into near-perpetual absolute rulers in their sphere of activity. The fact that teachers are under Civil Service is one of the most damning indictments against the American compulsory system of today.

To return to the first educationists, the main figures in the movement were such men as New Englanders Horace Mann in Massachusetts, and Henry Barnard in Connecticut. Also James Carter, Calvin Stowe, Caleb Mills, Samuel Lewis, and many others. What were their methods and their goals?

One of the methods to achieve their aims was to found a welter of interlocking educational organizations. One of the first was the American Lyceum, organized in 1826 by Josiah Holbrook. A major aim was to influence and to try to dominate state and local boards of education. In 1827, the first "Society for the Promotion of Public Schools" was opened in Pennsylvania. This society engaged in an extensive program of correspondence, pamphlets, press releases, etc. Similar organizations were formed in the early 1830s throughout the West, with lectures, meetings, memorials to legislatures, and lobbying featured. Hundreds of such associations formed throughout the land. One of the principal ones was the American Institute of Instruction, established in New England in 1830. The annual meetings and papers of this Institute were one of the leading clearing-houses and centers of educationist movements.

Secondly, the educationists formed educational journals by the dozens, through which the leading principles were disseminated to the followers. Principal ones were the *American Journal of Education*, the *American Annals of Education*, the *Common School Assistant*, and the *Common School Journal*. The most important route of educationist influence was obtaining leading positions in the state school systems. Thus, Horace Mann, editor of the *Common School Journal*, became secretary of the Massachusetts Board of Education, and his annual reports during the 1840s were extremely influential in setting the educationists' "line." Henry Barnard became Secretary of the Connecticut Board of Education, Calvin Wiley became head of the public schools in North Carolina, Caleb Mills in Indiana, Samuel Lewis in Ohio, etc.

The educationists, particularly under the influence of Horace Mann, did not go as far as advocating compulsory education. But they went up to that point in calling on everyone to go to the public schools, and in disparaging private schools. They were particularly eager to induce everyone to go to the public schools so that all might be molded in the direction of equality. Virginia's educationist Charles Mercer wrote a eulogy of the common school which it might be well to compare with Owen's plan:

> The equality on which our institutions are founded cannot be too intimately interwoven in the habits of thinking among our youth; and it is obvious that it would be greatly promoted by their continuance together, for the longest possible period; in the same schools of juvenile instruction; to sit upon the same forms; engage in the same competitions; partake of the same recreations and amusements, and pursue the same studies, in connection with each other; under the same discipline, and in obedience to the same authority.

And Mercer was the leader in Virginia's educationist movement. The vigorous championing of the public school's leveling role appeared again and again in the educationists' literature. Samuel Lewis particularly stressed that the common schools would take a diverse population and mold them into "one people;" Theodore Edson exulted that in such schools the good children must learn to mingle with the bad ones, as they will have to do in later life. The influential Orville Taylor, editor of the *Common School Assistant*, declared: "let all send to it (the common school); this is duty." And in 1837, words very much like Mercer's and Owen's:

> where high and low are taught in the same class, and out of the same book, and by the same teacher. This is a republican education.[19]

Hand in hand with such sentiments went disparagement of the private schools. This theme appeared almost universally in the educationist writings. James Carter stressed it in the 1820s; Orville

---

[19]*Common School Assistant*, vol. 2, 1837, p. 1. For Mercer's statement, see Charles Fenton Mercer, *A Discourse on Popular Education* (Princeton, 1826). Mercer's expression antedated Owen's. Also see the various annual lectures before the American Institute of Instruction.

Taylor declaimed in terms reminiscent of Owen that if a rich child is sent to a private school, he will be taught "that he is better than a public school child. This is not republicanism."

The educationists thought it essential to inculcate the children with moral principles, and this meant religious faith as well. They could not be sectarian, however, and still induce all the religious groups to send their children to public schools. Therefore, they decided to teach the fundamentals of Protestant Christianity in the public schools, as the common faith of everyone. This solution might not have been too glaring in the early period, but heavy immigration of Catholics soon after mid-century created insuperable difficulties in such a program. Another interesting facet of this period was an indication of the great limitation imposed on the educationists because instruction was still voluntary. Since parents could choose or not to send their children to the public schools, the teaching bureaucracy could not have full sway—the parents were still in control. Therefore, there could not be any religious absolutism. Furthermore, Horace Mann was emphatic in insisting that for all controversial political subjects, the teacher must be neutral. If he is not strictly neutral, then the parents of opposing views would not send their children to the public schools, and the ideal of uniform, equal education for all would be defeated.

Thus, we see the enormous importance of voluntary education as a check on tyranny. The public schools had to be kept politically as well as religiously neutral.[20] One basic flaw in this plan, of course, is that in dealing with political and economic subjects, it is almost impossible to treat them intelligently and accurately while being strictly neutral and avoiding all controversy. It is obviously the best plan, however, given the establishment of public schools.

The educationists chafed at these restrictions, and looked toward the Prussian model where these difficulties did not arise. Actually, they were only politically neutral where no great controversies existed, and they inculcated American nationalism and uniformity of language. Calvin Stowe urged adoption of the Prussian methods, although he claimed of course that in America the results would be republican and not despotic. Stowe urged the universal placing of school duty on the same plane as military

[20]Horace Mann's *Twelfth Annual Report*, p. 89.

duty. The influential Stowe spoke in almost the same terms, in 1836, as had Martin Luther three centuries before:

> If a regard to the public safety makes it right for a government to compel the citizens to do military duty when the country is invaded, the same reason authorizes the government to compel them to provide for the education of their children—for no foes are so much to be dreaded as ignorance and vice. A man has no more right to endanger the state by throwing upon it a family of ignorant and vicious children, than he has to give admission to spies of an invading army. If he is unable to educate his children the state should assist him—if unwilling, it should compel him. General education is as much certain, and much less expensive, means of defense, than military array.... Popular education is not so much a want as a duty...as education...is provided by the parents, and paid for by those who do not profit by its results, it is a duty.[21]

Another principle of the Prussian system which Stowe admired was its compulsory uniformity of language. He also praised its vigorous compulsory attendance and anti-truant laws.

Stowe's report on Prussian education was enormously influential among the educationists, and they took his lead on the subject. Mann and Barnard held similar views, although the former hesitated on compulsion. Barnard was not reluctant, however. Praising the Prussian educational system, he wrote:

> The regular attendance at the school shall be an object of specific control and the most active vigilance; for this is the source from which flow all the advantages the school can produce. It would be very fortunate if parents and children were always willing of themselves.... Unhappily, this is not the case, particularly in great cities. Although it is lamentable to be forced to use constraint, it is almost always necessary to commence with it.[22]

Horace Mann's sincerity was certainly open to question. In his annual reports, he denounced property rights, and talked of social control and the one Commonwealth's property. On the other hand, while asking for gifts from the industrialists for the schools, he

---

[21]Calvin E. Stowe, *The Prussian System of Public Instruction and its Applicability to the United States* (Cincinnati, 1830).

[22]Henry Barnard, *National Education in Europe* (New York, 1854).

abandoned this line and his talk of political neutrality, and declared that he thoroughly approved of indoctrination against Jacksonian democracy and mobocracy.[23] Henry Barnard also approved of indoctrination, for property as against mob rebellion. It is obvious that the educationists chafed hugely against the restraints of voluntarism. What was needed to permit State indoctrination and uniformity was the Prussian system of compulsion. This was adopted in the late nineteenth century, and the wraps were off; neutrality would no longer need to be imposed or claimed.

Another educationist declaration on behalf of State authority was made by the influential Josiah Quincy, Mayor of Boston and president of Harvard, who declared in 1848 that every child should be educated to obey authority. George Emerson, in 1873, asserted that it was very necessary for people to be accustomed from their earliest years to submit to authority. These comments were printed in leading educationist journals *Common School Journal* and *School and Schoolmaster*, respectively. The influential Jacob Abbott declared, in 1856, that a teacher must lead his students to accept the existing government. The Superintendent of Public Instruction of Indiana declared in 1853 that school policy was to mold all the people into one people with one common interest.

## Progressive Education and the Current Scene

It is obvious that there is little time or space here to enter into an extensive discussion of the much-criticized system of permissive–progressive education, and the state of current teaching in the public schools. Certain broad considerations, however, emerge, particularly in the light of the triumph of the Rousseau–Pestalozzi–Dewey system in this country since 1900:

(1) The effect of progressive education is to destroy independent thought in the child, indeed to repress any thought whatsoever. Instead, the children learn to revere certain heroic symbols (Gentile), or to follow the domination of the "group" (as in Lafcadio Hearn's *Japan*). Thus, subjects are taught as little as possible, and the child has little chance to develop any systematic reasoning powers in the study of definite courses. This program is being car-

---

[23]Compare Cremin, *The History of Compulsory Education in New England* and Curti, *The Social Ideas of American Educators.*

ried forward into high school, as well as grammar school, so that many high-school graduates are ignorant of elementary spelling or reading, and cannot write a cogent sentence. The ruling set of educationists are on the way to establishing colleges of this type, in which there would be no systematic courses, and have largely succeeded in the case of their teacher-training schools. The policy of letting the child "do what he likes" is an insidious one, since the children are encouraged to continue always at their original superficial level, without receiving guidance in study. Furthermore, the "three Rs," the fundamental tools, are neglected as long as possible, with the result that the child's chance to develop his mind is greatly retarded. The policy of teaching words via pictures instead of by the alphabet tends to deprive the young child of the greatest reasoning tool of all.

(2) Equality and uniformity are pursued more than ever, even under the guise of letting individuals do as they like. The plan is to abolish grades, by which better and worse children know the extent of their progress, and instead to grade "subjectively" or not at all. Subjective grading is a monstrous scheme to grade each student on the basis of what the teacher arbitrarily thinks the capacities of the child are, the grading to be rated on the extent to which the child fulfills these capacities. This places a terrible handicap on the bright students and grants special privileges to the moronic ones, who may get As if they are no more moronic than they truly are. Studies tend to be pursued now at the lowest common denominator, rather than at the average—so as not to "frustrate" the more moronic. As a result, the bright pupils are robbed of incentive or opportunity to study, and the dull ones are encouraged to believe that success, in the form of grades, promotions, etc., will come to them automatically.

Individuality is suppressed by teaching all to adjust to the "group." All emphasis is on the "group," and the group votes, runs its affairs by majority rule, etc. As a result, the children are taught to look for truth in the opinion of the majority, rather than in their own independent inquiry, or in the intelligence of the best in the field. Children are prepared for democracy by being led to discuss current events without first learning the systematic subjects (politics, economics, history) which are necessary in order to discuss them. The Mole effect is to substitute slogans and superficial opinion for considered individual thought. And the opinion is that of the lowest common denominator of the group.

It is clear that one of the major problems comes from the dullest group. The progressive educationists saw that the dullest could not be taught difficult subjects, or, indeed, simple subjects. Instead of drawing the logical conclusion of abandoning compulsory education for the uneducable, they decided to bring education down to the lowest level so that the dullest could absorb it—in fact, to move toward the elimination of subjects or grading altogether.

(3) The emphasis on "frills"—on physical education, play, and numerous trivial courses—again has the effect of being comprehensible to the most moronic, and hence insuring completely equal instruction for all. Furthermore, the more such subjects are emphasized, the less room there is for systematic thought.

(4) The idea that the school should not simply teach subjects, but should educate the "whole child" in all phases of life, is obviously an attempt to arrogate to the State all the functions of the home. It is an attempt to accomplish the molding of the child without actually seizing him as in the plans of Plato or Owen.

(5) Unquestionably, the effect of all this is to foster dependence of the individual on the group and on the State.

# Index